Jacob Pady, tenant of Sir William Pole at Whitwell Farm, Colyford, Colyton, Devon. He is seen here about 1900 with his second wife, Ellen, and his nine children, including Jack on horseback in the uniform of the Dorset Yeomanry.

THE
VICTORIAN FARMER

David J. Eveleigh

Shire Publications Ltd

CONTENTS

Printed in Great Britain by C. I. Thomas & Sons (Haverfordwest) Ltd, Press Buildings, Merlins Bridge, Haverfordwest, Dyfed SA61 1XF.

British Library Cataloguing in Publication Data: Eveleigh, David J. The Victorian farmer. 1. Great Britain. Agricultural industries, history. I. Title. 338.10941. ISBN 0-7478-0106-1.

ACKNOWLEDGEMENTS

Illustrations are acknowledged as follows: Beamish, pages 10 (bottom) and 13; Blaise Castle House Museum, pages 8, 9 (top), 16 (top left and bottom), 19, 24 (bottom left), 26 (top), 27, 29 (bottom) and 30 (left); Dr J. Brown, page 25 (bottom right); Tom and Bob Hignell, pages 4, 7 and 21 (top); Museum of English Rural Life, the cover and pages 1, 2, 3, 5, 6, 9 (bottom), 10 (top), all pictures on pages 11-12 and 14-15, 16 (top right), 17 (top and bottom), 18, 20, 21 (bottom), all pictures on pages 22-3, 24 (top and bottom right), 25 (top and bottom left), 26 (bottom), 28, 29 (top) and 30 (right).

Special thanks are due to Roy Brigden and the staff of the Museum of English Rural Life, Reading University; also to Andy Cotton, photographer at the City of Bristol Museum and Art Gallery, and to Greta Shiner for typing the manuscript.

Cover: *A farmer with his prize shorthorn at the Chichester Show in 1856. Oil on canvas by William Smith.*

Caricature of a farmer from 'Punch', 1843.

Farmer's son Arthur Barron on the horse and labourer 'Butt' Janson at White House Farm, North Ferriby, Humberside (formerly Yorkshire) in the 1890s.

INTRODUCTION

Who were the farmers of Victorian England? How did they live? There is no simple answer. The farmer was usually defined as 'the cultivator of the land'. The *Reading Observer* elaborated, somewhat partially, on this in 1880: 'The active and intelligent cultivator of the soil, the man who makes the rent, pays the rents and tithes and does all the work'. However, such definitions fail to take into account the tremendous diversity within the farming community. Ranging widely across the social spectrum, farmers could scarcely be described as a single social class. At one end were the gentlemen farmers, landowners, who cultivated a home or model farm on their own estates: the most celebrated was Prince Albert (1819-61), consort to Queen Victoria, who carried out extensive improvements on the royal estate at Windsor. At the other extreme were small farmers making a meagre living from as little as 5 acres (2 ha). In between

lay the largest and most important group, the overwhelming majority of whom were tenants of the great land-owners. If ever a typical farmer existed, he was in the last category.

At around 250,000, the total number of farmers in Queen Victoria's reign, from 1837 to 1901, changed little. Almost 90 per cent were tenants. Owner-occupiers were to be found only on the smallest holdings although the independent 'yeoman' farmer still existed in some counties. Paying rent to the landowners and providing employment for a huge population of landless agricultural labourers, the farmer's position in rural society was central. Furthermore, through the payment of tithes to the local parson and by forming an important clientele for village shopkeepers and tradesmen, farmers contributed more widely to the whole fabric of rural society.

Yet it was more than the working day which made the farmer. In the opinion of many Victorians, farming was not simply an occupation but a way of life, which, centred on the farmhouse, also required the participation of the farmer's wife and children: it was a family enterprise which inextricably bound work and the home. It was also a way of life often romanticised by writers. In 1838 William Howitt likened farmers to 'little kings', enjoying a healthier environment and exercising greater control over their surroundings than the tradesmen cramped in the towns and cities. Their home life was also much praised. The farmhouse was not short on comforts but neither was there any false show. William Cobbett summed it up simply in 1830 — 'plain manners and plentiful living'.

Such conventional pictures of farming life emphasised the traditional and unchanging, and farmers, notoriously conservative and slow to adopt new ideas, often confirmed the stereotype. Yet Victorian agriculture was far from static. Within this period occurred what some historians have termed the second agricultural revolution. The first, beginning in the mid eighteenth century, had been largely concerned with consolidating holdings through parliamentary enclosure and the introduction of new fodder crops. The second, beginning about 1840, was achieved through large-scale mechanisation and greater use of scientific methods. Allied to industry, agricultural progress brought the rural community into contact with a wider world. Aided by new advances in communications — the spread of railways and newspapers — new ideas reached all but the remotest farmhouses; inevitably the way of life for many farmers was to change.

Farming a family enterprise: Charles Britten with his family, c.1900. He held Minor's Farm, 78 acres (32 ha) at Hallen, Avon (formerly Gloucestershire).

The rent audit — paying rent to the landlord's agent: this took place at different times of the year according to the locality and was an occasion when all the tenants of an estate would meet to pay their rent and sometimes dine. By late Victorian times a farmer was more likely to pay by cheque. (From Jefferies Taylor, 'The Farm', 1832.)

THE FARMER AT WORK

The fortunes of most farmers, as tenants, were closely linked to the landed classes. The landed proprietors themselves varied: they could be local country gentlemen — the 'squirearchy' — or aristocrats like the Duke of Buccleuch, who owned extensive estates in six different counties. Generally the landlord provided fixed improvements — the buildings, fencing and field drainage — whilst the tenant provided the working capital. Farming, therefore, was a joint enterprise from which each stood to benefit. The tenant gained from the landlord's long-term investments whilst the landlord enjoyed the high rents generated by productive farming.

Whilst a good landlord realised it was in his interests to attract a good tenant, the farmer, equally, looked for security and commitment from the landowner. It was rare for a farmer to purchase his holding; this would only divert capital from the working operations. Some of the larger farms were held on agricultural leases — twenty years was common; these, it was argued, gave farmers the security to carry out long-term improvements on the land. But farmers and landowners alike were wary of fixing rent for a long period: the prices for farm produce were always fluctuating. Annual agreements, therefore, were almost universally preferred, providing for greater flexibility. They did, however, leave the farmer with little protection for his capital investment should he decide to leave. In some districts a tradition of tenant right operated, whereby the outgoing tenant was compensated for unexhausted improvements. But tenant right was not universal and even after 1875, when it was given legal sanction, disputes occasionally arose over the question of compensation.

Neglect on the part of the landlord was arguably a greater threat to good farming than the potential insecurity of tenure. Not all proprietors were as assiduous as the Dukes of Bedford or the Duke of Wellington in undertaking long-term improvements on their estates. In 1850, whilst surveying English agriculture, James Caird found the Duke of Wellington engaged in building substantial dwellings on his estate at Stratfield Saye in Hampshire; but this was in stark contrast to the rest of the county, where the general standard of accommodation provided by landlords was poor. In Suffolk, according to Caird, the tenants were left to erect farm buildings themselves. The result was insubstantial and inconvenient structures of wood and thatch. Neglect could sour relations between the two parties: in Leicestershire, where Caird found few improving landlords, distrust amongst the tenancy was rife. Disputes arose, too, from the damage to growing crops caused by the landlord's hunting rights. But such difficulties tended to be local rather than national and generally landowners and farmers enjoyed good relations — the latter joining in the hunt whenever the opportunity arose! In spite of the apparent impermanence of annual agreements, many farms remained in the same family for generations, passed down from father to son; such continuity fostered a close relationship between the two groups and many tenants loyally followed their landlord's lead in local and political affairs.

Beyond the ubiquity of tenancies there was little in common amongst so variable and diverse a class. Natural conditions, economic circumstances and traditions varied over Britain and so in turn did the

A farmer enjoying the hunt, even though it meant riding over his own crop. Original caption: Member of hunt (to farmer), 'I wouldn't ride over those seeds if I were you. They belong to a disagreeable sort of fellow who might make a fuss about it.' Farmer, 'Well, Sir, as him's me, he won't say nothing about it today.' ('Punch', 1st April, 1876.)

The working farmer: Clement Hignell (on wagon), a tenant farmer, loading hay at Lawrence Weston Farm, 128 acres (52 ha), Avon (formerly Gloucestershire), on 6th July 1904. This farm is now submerged beneath suburban Bristol.

size and condition of the farms. Most fell within the 100-300 acre (40-120 ha) range although in the south and east there were arable farms considerably larger than this — as much as 2000 acres (800 ha) on the Lincolnshire Wolds. In the west, where pastoral farming predominated, holdings were generally smaller. Some dairy farms comprised only 20 acres (8 ha) but farms smaller still were not uncommon; they were often held by butchers, carters or other village tradesmen who supplemented their income with a little farming. In the West Riding of Yorkshire hand-loom weavers frequently combined their business with farming. These weaver-farmers seldom made much money but small farmers could be successful, particularly where a town provided a ready market for dairy produce and vegetables; generally, however, it was the larger farms which yielded the greatest profits.

Inevitably, there was little in common between the prosperous farmer with 500 acres (200 ha) or more at his disposal and the man trying to make a living from 20 acres (8 ha) and a few dairy cows. Both were farmers but between the two was a huge gulf in ideas, abilities and lifestyle.

500 acres (200 ha) was considered the threshold for upper middle-class living and large farmers, some holding more than one farm, pursued lives scarcely distinguishable from those of the land-owners. Indeed, such farmers mixed freely with them, sharing the pleasures of the hunt and doing no manual work themselves. Typically, these farmers were educated men, forward thinking, ready to place their faith and their capital in new farming techniques. The Royal Agricultural Society of England and the Farmer's Club were both creations of this age, founded in 1838 and 1844 respec-

7

Farmhouse for bailiff and stables designed by George Godwin, built in 1855 at Stanley Farm, north of Bristol. This and the neighbouring Walls Court Farm were run as one unit of some 600 acres (250 ha) by Thomas Proctor, a Bristol fertiliser manufacturer who invested heavily in new farming techniques. ('The Builder', 3rd March 1860.)

tively. At their meetings and shows the progressive farmer would discuss new ideas, attend lectures and with a critical eye gauge the performance of the latest farm machinery. The Victorian revolution in agriculture was due in no small measure to the enterprise of these men.

Yet for every progressive farmer there were many more who lacked the resources to embark on improvements. They were usually the smaller farmers — that is, with fewer than 100 acres (40 ha); they worked in the fields alongside their men; they were also often deeply conservative in their ways and suspicious of new ideas. Such were the near-illiterate farmers James Caird encountered in 1850 on the Surrey clays and in Sussex using cumbersome old-fashioned wooden ploughs drawn by teams of oxen. Entrenched in tradition, small farmers were still found at the end of the nineteenth century. In 1892 J. K. Fowler, a rich and successful gentleman farmer from the vale of Aylesbury, spoke of the 50 acre (20 ha) man on the Chiltern Hills, in his

smock frock, barely distinguishable from the farm labourer. For these farmers, making a living was a constant and difficult struggle, 'going on', said Fowler, borrowing the local vernacular, 'from cherry time to cherry time and getting no forwarder'.

Farmers' circumstances, moreover, varied over time and from district to district. The vicissitudes of the harvest and fluctuations in prices and markets exerted a considerable influence on the well-being of the farming classes. For the greater part of the nineteenth century the price of corn seemingly dominated the agricultural climate. Victoria's reign began with farming in a state of depression: low grain prices prevailed, in spite of the 1815 Corn Law (modified in 1828), which aimed to protect the British farmer from low prices by forbidding the sale of foreign grain until the home price rose to 80 shillings (£4) a quarter (12.7 kg). The low prices were largely caused by the increased acreage brought under cultivation during the Napoleonic Wars and by higher yields, the result of improved techniques: with agricultural output matching the growth of consumption, prices were bound to fall. The role of the Corn Laws, therefore, was clearly exaggerated, yet landowners and farmers firmly believed that they were vital for the prosperity of British agriculture; at the same time they were bitterly opposed by the supporters of free trade — industrialists and political radicals who formed the Anti Corn Law League in 1838. When, in 1846, the Prime Minister, Sir Robert Peel, gave way to the free-traders and repealed the laws, it was widely feared in the countryside that depression would follow. For a short while, as prices fell, it seemed their fears were to be realised, but from the early 1850s there followed two decades of prosperity, the years of 'high farming' — the golden age of Victorian agriculture.

Buoyed by high prices and expanding

Above right: *Farmers, so often portrayed by opponents of the Corn Laws as rustic dullards, had predicted widespread distress would follow the repeal of the laws. By the mid 1850s, however, farmers were enjoying prosperous times. Original caption: Farmer, 'Well here's a pretty business! I've got so much corn that I don't know where to put it.' ('Punch', 9th September 1854.)*

Below: *Old-fashioned farming: ploughing at Homedean Farm, Lewes, East Sussex, in April 1888 with a heavy wooden turn-rest plough.*

Farming with steam was a Victorian innovation: steam ploughing with a Kitson and Hewitson engine and tackle, 1862.

markets, high farming was typified by high productivity, producing the highest output per acre through the application of new techniques — in field drainage, flexible crop rotation, the use of artificial fertilisers and new machinery. It was in farm equipment that the advances were most impressive: iron displaced wood in the manufacture of many field implements and from the 1840s steam was established as a practical form of power on the farm for threshing, driving barn machinery and, to a lesser extent, ploughing. A new breed of farmer emerged: an industrialist at heart who saw farming less as a way of life than as a business. Such was Richard Jefferies's 'Man of Progress', based on E. Taylor Middleditch of Baydon near Swindon, on whose farm 'the beat of the engines never

Break time whilst threshing with steam in Lingdale, Cleveland (formerly Yorkshire), c.1870. The man leaning against the cart on the right is probably the farmer.

seemed to cease'. Another pioneering figure was Joseph Mechi (1801-80), a London businessman of Italian origin who took over a run-down farm at Tiptree, Essex, in 1841. Through heavy investment in new farm buildings, steam-powered machinery and field drainage Mechi doubled the productivity of his land.

In the 1860s, however, Mechi ran into financial difficulties and ultimately went bankrupt shortly before his death. High farming was effective only on farms larger than 300 acres (120 ha), and Tiptree Farm totalled only 130 acres (53 ha). It was also profitable only so long as prices remained high enough to support the high levels of investment and when, after 1875, prices fell depression quickly followed. The golden age was over. As contemporaries sought an answer to the slump, attention turned to the lifestyle of farmers: had they perhaps contributed to their downfall by living beyond their means?

Above: *John Joseph Mechi (1801-80) amassed a fortune as a cutler in Leadenhall Street, London, before entering farming. These commercial interests in the City contributed to his later difficulties.*

Below: *Farm mechanisation transformed harvesting. By 1890 roughly 80 per cent of the British corn area was cut by machine, greatly reducing labour requirements at harvest time. After about 1870 machines for cutting grass like this 'Buckeye' mower also became widespread. ('Ironmonger', October 1874.)*

The farmyard at Sulham Farm near Pangbourne, Berkshire, in 1884.

An old farmhouse at Westcott, Surrey; timber-framing infilled with brick, and a thatched roof, c.1900-5.

A stone-built farmhouse with thatched roof at High Horsleyhope Farm, Derwentside, Durham, 1890-1900.

THE FARMER AT HOME

The lifestyle of farmers varied according to the size and income of their holdings. It was seen in their dress, diet, how they spent their leisure time and, above all, in the home, for the farmhouse was the clearest visible expression of the farmer's way of life. Like farms, farmhouses varied in size, but they also varied immensely in outward appearance and almost as much in their internal layout. There were, nevertheless, common characteristics which set farmhouses apart from other homes.

Some farmers inhabited old houses dating back several centuries. Occasionally, these incorporated medieval structures; others had been built during prosperous times in the sixteenth and seventeenth centuries; some were old manor houses which had come down in the world. These older dwellings — earlier, that is, than about 1720 — were found in all counties but varied considerably in appearance. They had been built to no published architectural rules but according to vernacular tradition. Local styles

abounded and building materials were those ready to hand. In areas of good building stone they closely reflected the underlying geology: sandstones, grits and limestones according to the locality. Elsewhere, a tradition of timber-framed building infilled with wattle and daub or brick predominated. Roofs were often thatched.

The plan of older farmhouses, complicated in many instances by later alterations and extensions, was often rambling and inconvenient It was common for them to be set in the midst of the working farm buildings so that the farmer and his family lived cheek by jowl with the sights, sounds and smells of the farmyard. Their old-fashioned interiors fascinated visitors: the immense kitchens, the dark staircases, long passages and flagstone floors. Adored by romantics, they were, nevertheless, the despair of progressive agriculturalists, who argued that inconvenient dwellings would not attract good tenants.

Less quaint although far superior in the

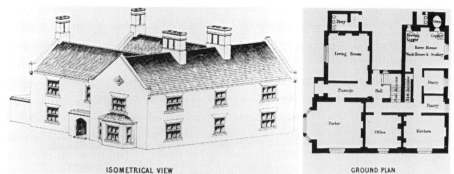

ISOMETRICAL VIEW   GROUND PLAN

A farmhouse for a mixed farm of 500 acres (200 ha) erected by the Earl Spencer at Boddington, Northamptonshire. Designed by John Beasley of Chapel Brampton, Northamptonshire, it was built of stone and roofed with Welsh slates. (J. Bailey Denton, 'The Farm Homesteads of England', 1855.)

accommodation they offered were the farmhouses built in the late eighteenth and early nineteenth centuries as a result of enclosure. At the centre of newly laid-out farms smart new farmhouses were constructed. In the Midland counties, where this period of enclosure transformed the landscape, they were particularly common, conspicuous by their neat Georgian façades in brick with roofs of tile or slate. The architecture was fashionable, not vernacular, and some were substantial enough to be mistaken for the homes of gentlemen.

Then another spate of building and rebuilding occurred between 1830 and 1880. The design and layout were heavily influenced by the specimen plans of farmsteads produced by architects such as Francis Goodwin, J. C. Loudon and J. Bailey Denton. Improving landowners realised that to attract tenants with sufficient capital to invest in the larger farms it was necessary to provide well arranged

A farmhouse kitchen at Brotherikeid Farm, Eskdale, Cumbria (formerly Westmorland), c.1890s.

farm buildings and a well appointed house. Thus Bailey Denton related his designs not simply to farm size but to the amount of tenant capital required to run the farm effectively. On the largest farms the result was the construction of sumptuous farmhouses, especially during the years of high farming; many more modest dwellings, besides, were completely rebuilt. The styles varied although 'Rural Gothic' and 'Old English', reviving elements of vernacular architecture, predominated. The quaint and picturesque exteriors of these farmhouses with their steeply pitched roofs, gables and ornate chimneys often belied the modern thinking behind their internal layout.

Regardless of outward style, age and size, all farmhouses divided into service and living areas, the former including rooms for brewing, baking, dairying and laundering, and the latter represented by at least a parlour. Bridging the two and serving as the focal point of farmhouse life was the kitchen, where all occupants would meet. In some areas unmarried farmworkers or servants lodged with the farmers, sleeping in attic bedrooms and eating in the kitchen. In southern England this custom had largely died out by the beginning of Victoria's reign but on farms in the north and west it survived throughout. In the mid nineteenth century some farmhouses on the Yorkshire Wolds contained as many as twenty people. The farmhouse kitchen was generally large and spacious — as much as 30 feet (9 metres) long and nearly as wide. The walls were usually whitewashed, the floors of brick or stone flags; Hyppolite Taine, a Frenchman who visited several farmhouses near London in 1861, found the cleanliness of the interiors 'altogether Dutch' in character. The kitchen was dominated by the fireplace, often large enough to accommodate an oven and space for smoking hams. Attracted by the warmth and light, members of the household would gather around the fire and here the farmer's wife would cook their meals.

The furniture of the kitchen embodied Cobbett's 'plain manners': it was simple and functional — the product of the village joiner working to local traditions. Styles scarcely changed; only the increas-

ing use of imported deal in place of native oak, ash and elm distinguished newer articles. Certain items were basic to all kitchens: a robust, long table, for example, large enough to seat all the household. Chairs of ladder-back or spindle-back construction with rush seats were common, as were Windsor chairs. Distinguished by their fluid lines, the key to their success, Windsor chairs had first appeared in the early eighteenth century. By the mid nineteenth century several styles had evolved besides the basic comb-back type: bow-backs and scroll-backs, smokers' bows and one particularly substantial lath-back with heavy turnings and arms which was popularly known as the farmhouse Windsor. Alternative seating was provided by the settle, which was invariably placed beside the fire, where its back served as a screen against the cutting draughts drawn up the chimney. Purely functional settles often incorporated lockers under the seat and some had cupboards in the back for storing hams. Another essential item was the kitchen dresser, the shelves frequently adorned with the cheap Staffordshire blue and white earthenware which by Victorian times had replaced pewter

A stone sink and pump at Lord's Leaze Farm, Chard, Somerset.

15

No. 544

Very Strong Arm Chair, Lath back ... 15/6 18/-
Birch or Cherry Wood, 22/6 25/-. Large size, 25/- 30/-
Similar Chair, plain Spindles in back ... 10/6 12/6

Above left: *Lath-back Windsor armchair. (Catalogue of Laverton and Company, Bristol, 1875.)*

Above right: *A pine settle made c.1880 for the farmhouse kitchen at Lord's Leaze Farm, Chard, Somerset. The settle was grained in dark red-brown and had cupboards in the back.*

Left: *A nineteenth-century pine dresser, 5 feet (1.5 metres) wide, in the kitchen of a farmhouse at East Dundry, Avon (formerly Somerset.)*

Rich and fashionable furnishings in the dining room of a farmhouse at Writtle, Essex; watercolour, 1863.

as the main type of tableware. Other furnishings included corner cupboards, bread creels or bacon racks suspended from the ceiling and long-case clocks. Each kitchen would also contain innum-

erable smaller articles of everyday use: wooden pattens (overshoes worn by women to keep their long skirts above the wet), guns, wooden mousetraps, fire irons and candlesticks of steel and brass,

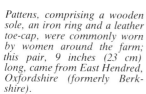

Pattens, comprising a wooden sole, an iron ring and a leather toe-cap, were commonly worn by women around the farm; this pair, 9 inches (23 cm) long, came from East Hendred, Oxfordshire (formerly Berkshire).

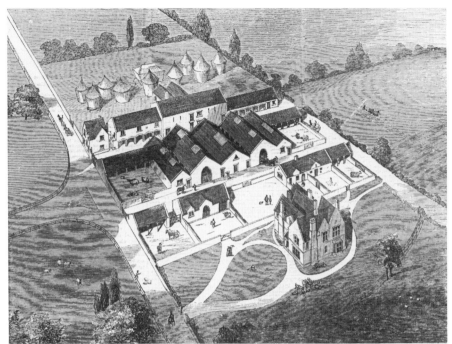

In this steading designed by William Wilkinson in 1858 for a 600 acre (240 ha) farm on the Duke of Marlborough's estate in Oxfordshire the farmhouse turns its back on the working buildings, facing south over landscaped gardens. ('Illustrated London News', 18th December 1858.)

these by degrees reflecting the light of the fire.

If the kitchen maintained the old-fashioned and traditional, the other living areas were more likely to reflect the varying levels of wealth and the social aspirations of their occupants. Even the humblest farmhouses included a parlour, a best room set aside where the farmer and his immediate family could relax in some privacy. According to J. C. Loudon, author of the influential *Cottage, Farm and Villa Architecture*, first published in 1833, the furnishings of living rooms of working farmers ought to be 'substantial and rather plain' lest they should be soiled by their 'thick and earth stained shoes'. A glimpse of the interior of one of these rooms in a modest farmhouse near Hereford is provided by Frederick Olmstead, an American farmer, in 1850. He entered the parlour, a 'small room, neatly furnished': there

were 'painted deal chairs, a printed calico covered lounge'; the walls, he noted, were papered, the floors carpeted, but there were no books other than a Bible and an old almanac.

The large farmer, progressive in his work and equally so in his home life, sought to live in surroundings equal to his immediate social superiors. Loudon conceded this — 'of course the wealthy farmer may have his drawing room as highly finished and highly furnished as the independent landowner.' For successful farmers to live like country gentlemen was not new; it had been noticed, and indeed condemned, ever since the late eighteenth century. But what was new in Victorian times was the increasing tendency of socially ambitious farmers to model their lifestyle on the urban middle class. The emergence of this class as an important and influential section of British society was itself largely a Victorian phenomenon. They were distinguished by their own clearly defined values: above all, the importance of respectable family life and the desire for privacy; and these, aided by improved communications, spread to their rural counterparts.

One consequence was evident in the location of new farmhouses. Whereas only a generation earlier these were arranged so that the farmer could at all times view operations from indoors, they now generally turned their back on the farmyard. Instead, the principal living rooms looked out over formal front gardens. Another consequence was that farmers withdrew from the rough co-existence of the kitchen in preference for a more private family life in their own rooms. Work and home were now physically detached.

Amongst affluent farmers the parlour even went into a slight decline, being replaced by the drawing room. Taine entered one of these in 1861 on a large farm of 600 acres (240 ha) near London.

The splendour of the furnishings amazed him: 'large curtains supported by gilded poles, two elegant and well furnished mirrors, tasteful armchairs, in the middle a table covered with pretty volumes'. New farmhouses sometimes included a second drawing room, less formal than the first, as well as a dining room, study and even a library. Their furnishings were equally opulent, as notices of farm sales confirmed: in 1879 the *Reading Observer* advertised the sale by auction of Manor Farm, Bix, near Henley-on-Thames, Oxfordshire, including 'modern' furniture for drawing, dining and bed rooms. Also in 1879, a few miles away at Soundess Farm, Nettlebed, the sale included a drawing-room suite of walnut, a bookcase, a mahogany sideboard, a piano and a 'handsome barometer and thermometer'. This conspicuous consumption was far removed from the plain and simple farmers of popular imagination; it was evidence to some that they and their families were living too extravagantly.

The plainly dressed farmer of 1839 contrasted with the fashionably attired farmer of 1879. ('Punch', 13th March 1880.)

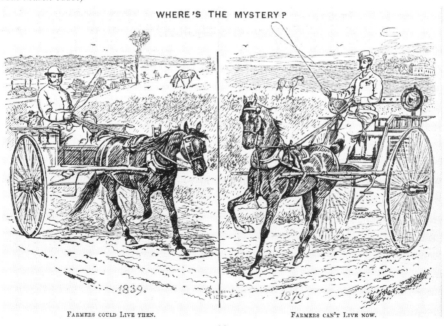

WHERE'S THE MYSTERY?

1839.   1879.

FARMERS COULD LIVE THEN.   FARMERS CAN'T LIVE NOW.

A farmer's wife and farmyard stock on a farm near Wincanton, Somerset, c.1900.

THE FARMER'S WIFE

It was a common maxim of Victorian farming that if a man was to farm land as a matter of business he would require the assistance of a business wife. In early Victorian England this was true of all but the largest holdings; on smaller farms the entire family often bore the brunt of the farm work, employing only one or two labourers. But the farmer's wife occupied a special role, not only contributing to the farm income through managing the dairy, feeding the poultry and even occasionally assisting with the heavier manual work, but also being charged with the major responsibility of running the household.

Most farmhouses had a dairy as milk, butter and cream were widely produced, if only for domestic consumption. On the home farms of landowners dairies were often showpieces of architectural ornamentation, but farmhouse dairies were usually plainer, with the same white-washed walls and paved floors as the other work areas. Normally one room had to make do for the cream settling and butter churning; a northerly aspect and leaded or louvred ventilators ensured that the cool environment essential for making butter was maintained.

Cheese was not as widely made as butter: it was more complex and required more equipment. Nevertheless, it was made even in counties such as Essex and Suffolk where its reputation was not high. On dairy farms in Cheshire, where cheese formed three-quarters of the total produce, the farmer's wife was the most important person in the establishment. The dairies of these farms could be quite extensive: at Broxton Farm, near Tattenhall, the dairy comprised a kitchen, scullery, a cheese press and drying room, a milk room, a pantry and a shed for storing vessels. Dairy work was exacting,

Above: *The farmer's daughter, Ivy Britten, feeding poultry at Minor's Farm, Hallen, Avon (formerly Gloucestershire), c.1912.*

Right: *Working the butter to remove the butter-milk at Riplington Farm, East Meon, Hampshire, 1908-10.*

demanding long hours, much personal attention, high standards of hygiene, skill and experience. But it was not always profitable. In 1850 Caird reckoned that the farmers' wives and families on the Cheshire dairy farms worked harder than almost anywhere else but for all their hard work and frugal living made little money. In northern and western counties the farmer's wife further contributed to the farm income by attending country markets. Besides dairy produce, she would sell poultry, eggs, fruit, flowers, honey and jam. It was a welcome break from the heavy routine of farmhouse work, a social occasion when she could meet other farmers' wives, settle accounts and buy a few things for the home.

Within doors the duties of the farmer's

Above left: *A farmhouse dairy: the dairymaid is pouring the milk into cream settling pans. (Jefferies Taylor, 'The Farm', 1832.)*

Above right: *An iron and brass skimmer used on the farm of Joseph and Mary Ann Turner, farmers and cheesemakers, on the Causeway, Mark, Somerset; handle 16½ inches (42 cm) long, diameter 7 inches (18 cm).*

Below: *The cheesemaking room at Windmill Farm, Blunsdon, Wiltshire, c.1890. Mrs Evans, the farmer's wife, ran the cheesemaking until the farm was sold in 1896. She produced about 120 pounds (54 kg) of Cheddar cheese per day, much of which was sold wholesale in Bristol.*

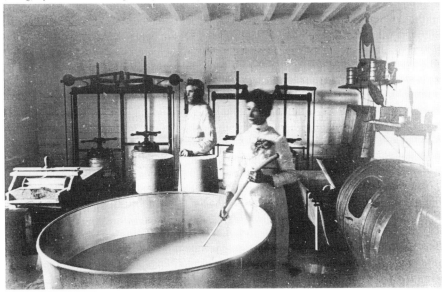

Above: *Two dairymaids standing beside a butter-working table, with a barrel butter churn to the left, at Whitleas Farm near Blanchland, Northumberland, c.1900.*

Below: *A coopered strainer used for brewing on a farm at Great Cornard, Suffolk, until 1932.*

wife were considerable and demanded a wide range of traditional domestic skills. Many farms existed as isolated, self-contained communities: self-sufficiency was part of the way of life. Many essential foodstuffs and other commodities were prepared by the farmer's wife; only the brewing and the making of cider were generally left to the men. Bread was a major part of the diet and farms often baked their own. Yeast left over from the brewing was added to dough, which was left to rise by the fire in a large earthenware bowl, a 'pancheon', while the oven was heated in readiness. By the 1830s over much of the north cast iron ovens with integral grates, flues and dampers were common, but elsewhere the farmer's wife still relied on the traditional brick oven heated by burning faggots inside. Raking out the hot ashes, gauging the temperature and loading the oven by balancing the dough on a long-handled peel required a deft touch and experience. Bread was usually baked weekly,

23

Above: *Making cider at Henage Farm, Medhurst, Chobham, Surrey, in 1907.*

Below left: *A nineteenth-century cast iron oven door from the Coalbrookdale foundry, Shropshire, in a farmhouse at East Dundry, Avon (formerly Somerset).*

Below right: *A wooden oven peel.*

24

A chopper used on a farm at Great Cornard, Suffolk, for cutting up pigs' carcases.

along with cakes, pastries and puddings.

Farms also generally cured their own bacon and hams to provide meat throughout the year. Killing the pig was a great annual event, usually done in November. After a lengthy process of drying and salting, which varied regionally, the flitches were smoked in the kitchen chimney or hung from the ceiling. Fruits grown by the farmer's wife in her kitchen garden were also preserved, in jams, pickles and wines.

Probably the most time-consuming job for most farmers' wives was the daily routine of preparing meals for all those living in the farmhouse. The fare was characteristically plain but substantial, with plenty of meat, eggs, dairy produce and vegetables when in season. There was a strong regional flavour to many of the dishes, prepared to traditional recipes. It was generally acknowledged

Left: *An iron tea kettle with a tilting device riveted to the handle. From Bangrove Farm in the Vale of Tewkesbury, Gloucestershire.*

Right: *An open fireplace with chimney crane, firedogs and iron hearth oven in the kitchen of a farmhouse at Woodley near Reading, probably built around 1800 and now demolished.*

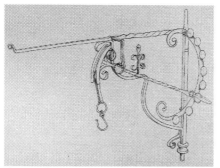

A wrought iron chimney crane from a farm near Newport, Essex.

that farm labourers who lodged with the farmer enjoyed a far superior diet to those living separately. In the 1840s, in East Yorkshire farmhouses, the workforce ate plenty of beef, bacon, meat pies and apple dumplings and in 1851 Caird reported that in Cumberland the labourers, married and single, received all their food in the farmer's kitchen: broth, meat and bread for dinner, and bread, porridge and milk for breakfast and supper. The same year, in Derbyshire, at Burchill's Farm on the Duke of Devonshire's estate near Bakewell, Caird found the men enjoying a substantial diet of porridge, bread and cheese for breakfast, bacon, beef or mutton with pudding and small beer for lunch, and at 7pm a supper

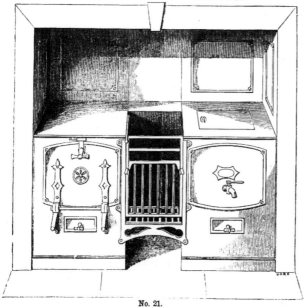

FARM KITCHEN RANGE.

No. 21.

Having all the Improvements of the Prize Cottage Range, but made in larger sizes.

SIZES AND PRICES OF FARM RANGE.

	3 ft. 8 in.	4 ft.	4 ft. 3 in.	4 ft. 9 in.	5 ft. 3 in.
Width of Fire............	10 in.	11 in.	12 in.	13 in.	14 in.
Size of Oven and Boiler....	14 in.	15 in.	16 in.	18 in.	20 in.
Price, with Tap......	£4 7 0	5 14 0	7 7 0	10 0 0	14 0 0
If with Covings, add......	1 1 0	1 3 0	1 7 0	1 12 0	2 0 0
If with Brass Handles, add..	0 3 0	0 3 6	0 4 0	0 4 6	0 5 0

A farmhouse kitchen range with open fire, oven and boiler advertised by S. and E. Ransome and Company, London, January 1858.

26

of milk, porridge, bread and cheese. 'The men', added Caird, 'are stout and muscular and work hard.' In southern England the farmer's wife had to cater only for her immediate family; the labourers lived by a meagre diet in their own cottages and there the gulf in lifestyle between the farmhouse and cottage was more pronounced.

Meals were cooked at the large kitchen fireplace. Fuel, therefore, was an important part of the rural economy, wood, coal, peat or furze being used according to the locality. In early Victorian times the price of coal remained high away from the coalfields and over large parts of Britain wood or turf continued to be burned on the open hearth. Cooking was carried out amongst the embers or in vessels suspended from wrought iron hangers or chimney cranes fashioned by the local blacksmith. Where coal was used, as in Derbyshire, Yorkshire and Durham, the fireplace contained a grate or range often with an oven and boiler. The spread of railways in the 1850s and 1860s brought cheaper coal to many areas and coal-burning ranges were fitted into many more farmhouses. The ranges, products in the main of the industrial towns of the Midlands, the north and Scotland, were themselves brought to hitherto isolated rural districts by the new railways. Improved communications brought other new consumer goods from the manufacturing districts: domestic utensils of cast iron, galvanised and enamelled iron from the Black Country and oil lamps from Birmingham. In isolated districts farmers' wives still made candles and rushlights from tallow and kitchen fat produced on the farm but from 1859 simple lamps burning cheap paraffin oil appeared and these were soon widely adopted in rural homes. By the 1870s the material world of the Victorian town was fast gaining a hold within the farmhouse.

In the second half of the nineteenth century some of the traditional tasks of the farmer's wife declined in importance. By the 1850s the home baking of bread was waning, especially in the south, where a century earlier village bakers had first appeared. Domestic baking survived longer in the Midlands and north; in the

A farmer from Penarch, Powys, peeling a rush for domestic lighting in 1913.

south only Suffolk and Devon maintained a reputation for home-baked bread after 1850. Similarly, brewing declined — dramatically between 1850 and 1875. By the 1870s the old custom of paying the workforce partly in kind, often including a beer allowance, was giving way to a full money wage. The dairy was also declin-

27

The kitchen of a farmhouse at Sibford Ferris, Oxfordshire, in 1916. A small range has been fitted in the former open fireplace and a paraffin lamp hangs over the table.

ing in importance. From the 1880s cheap imports of butter and cheese encouraged many farmers to turn to sending milk by rail to the towns.

However, if on some farms the business role of the farmer's wife was contracting, contemporary comment was louder against those who would no longer work. During the years of high farming the families of many medium-sized and larger farms were influenced by new urban fashions. Farmers' wives and daughters fashionably attired in clothes wholly unsuited for work around the farm attracted comment. In 1861 Taine was struck by the beauty and elegance of the wife of a farmer of 600 acres (240 ha) near London. She received him 'in a dress of small striped grey silk with one or two rings on her fingers, perfectly white hands, pink and cared for nails'. Such women rejected their traditional role in favour of a leisured routine of needlework, painting and playing the piano. When agricultural depression set in after 1875, the piano was taken by some to symbolise all that was wrong with the farming community: 'Has not some of the old stubborn spirit of earnest work and careful prudence gone with the advent of the piano and the oil painting?' asked Richard Jefferies in 1880.

Turning their backs on the farmyard visible through the window of this smartly furnished farmhouse living room at Writtle, Essex, the farmer's children spend their time reading, writing and sewing; watercolour, 1863.

Times change: a fashionably attired farmer's daughter asserts that she would rather play the piano and 'go for a gov'ness' than help in the dairy as her mother had done when she was young ('Punch', 11th April 1885).

Left: *Original caption: Jonathan, 'They du say we sent you this darn'd weather. Don't know 'bout that, anyhow, I guess we'll send you the corn!!' Farmer Bull, 'Thank'ee kindly Jonathan but I'd rather ha' done without both!!!' A comment on the difficulties of 1879. ('Punch', 6th September 1879.)*

Right: *Little of the traditional deference of farmers to landowners is evident in this cartoon. Original caption: Landlord (to tenant who had given up farming at the end of his lease to await better times), 'Well, Jackson, how do you like living on your capital?' Farmer, 'Not too well, my lord; but I find it cheaper than letting you live on it!' ('Punch', 30th August 1879.)*

CONCLUSION

The golden age of Victorian farming came to an abrupt end in 1875 and a long depression set in, lasting for the rest of the century. Its causes absorbed contemporaries. Richard Jefferies articulated the opinions of those who saw the personal extravagance of farmers as the chief cause of their distress; there was little sympathy for farmers who complained they could not make ends meet when they lived so well. But the fashionable farmer was probably only ever found on the larger farms; many farmers remained untouched by the attractions of Victorian consumerism.

Farmers themselves were inclined to blame the weather, which deteriorated markedly from 1875. Several wet seasons and poor harvests in succession culminated in the particularly wet summer of 1879, when every type of farming was affected. Worst hit were the large cereal farmers: low yields failed to raise prices and the high investments typical of these farms could not be maintained. The growing imports of cheap grain from abroad were the fundamental problem. Free trade was finally making itself felt. Some farmers were able to withstand the worst effects of the recession: the milk trade and horticulture both benefited from the growth of the railways, which brought remote farms into contact with urban markets. Many farmers, however, decided to quit and from the late 1870s there was a marked increase in farm

30

sales. Some managed to get out early with their capital intact; others stayed on, hoping for better times, but there were also bankruptcies.

By 1900 many old-established farming families had gone. They were replaced, in Essex, for instance, by families from northern England, Scotland and the West Country who made a success of farming by drastically reducing costs, working in the fields themselves and accepting a lower standard of living. The greater turnover of tenants reduced the old ties between landlord and tenant; the old order in the countryside was breaking up. It was also a much diminished community. If railways brought many benefits to farmers, they also took away their best labourers, attracted by better prospects in the towns. Farmers, therefore, lost their position as major employers. Whilst their numbers remained virtually unchanged, the number of agricultural labourers dropped: between 1871 and 1911 the proportion of the national workforce engaged in agriculture nearly halved.

Interest in the countryside from an overwhelmingly urban population increased in late Victorian Britain. Painters, poets, writers — and photographers, a sign of changing times — sought out the old-style farmer. But the reality was more complex than any idealised stereotype. Agriculturalists demanded progress of farmers; popular opinion called for tradition. The truth was that farmers as a body were at once a curious mix of both modern and old-fashioned.

FURTHER READING

Brigden, R. D. *Victorian Farms*. Crowood, 1986.
Caird, J. *English Agriculture in 1850-51*. Longman, 1852.
Denton, J. Bailey. *The Farm Homesteads of England*. Chapman and Hall, 1855.
Fowler, J. K. *Echoes of Old Country Life*. Edward Arnold, 1892.
Haggard, H. Rider. *A Farmer's Year*. Longman, 1899.
Howitt, W. *The Rural Life of England*. Longman, 1839.
Jefferies, R. *Hodge and his Masters*. Smith Elder, 1880.
Loudon, J. C. *Cottage, Farm and Villa Architecture*. Longman, 1833.
Mingay, G. E. *Rural Life in Victorian England*. Heinemann, 1977.
Mingay, G. E. (editor). *The Victorian Countryside*. Routledge Kegan Paul, 1981.
Olmstead, F. L. *Walks and Travels of an American Farmer in England*. University of Michigan Press, 1852 and 1968.
Perry, P. J. *British Farming in the Great Depression 1870-1914*. David and Charles, 1974.
Peters, J. E. C. *Discovering Traditional Farm Buildings*. Shire, 1981.
Taine, H. *Notes on England*. Stahan, 1872.
Ward, S. *Seasons of Change*. George Allen and Unwin, 1982.

PLACES TO VISIT

Intending visitors are advised to find out the times of opening before making a special journey.

Acton Scott Working Farm Museum, Wenlock Lodge, Acton Scott, Church Stretton, Shropshire SY6 6QN. Telephone: 06946 306 or 307.

Beamish: The North of England Open Air Museum, Beamish, Stanley, County Durham DH9 0RG. Telephone: 0207 231811.

Bishop's Waltham Palace, Bishop's Waltham, Hampshire. Telephone: 0489 892460. English Heritage. 1860s farmhouse kitchen display.

Cogges Farm Museum, Church Lane, Cogges, Witney, Oxfordshire OX8 6LA. Telephone: 0993 772602.

Cotswold Countryside Collection, Fosseway, Northleach, Cheltenham, Gloucestershire GL54 3JH. Telephone: (summer) 0451 60715; (winter) 0285 655611.

Dorset County Museum, High West Street, Dorchester, Dorset DT1 1XA. Telephone: 0305 262735.

Folk Museum of West Yorkshire, Shibden Hall, Halifax, West Yorkshire HX3 6XG. Telephone: 0422 352246.

The Great Barn, Avebury, Marlborough, Wiltshire SN8 1RF. Telephone: 06723 555.

Hampshire Farm Museum, Manor Farm, Brook Lane, Botley, Hampshire SO3 2ER. Telephone: 0489 787055.

Museum of English Rural Life, The University, Whiteknights, Reading, Berkshire RG6 2AG. Telephone: 0734 318660.

Museum of Kent Rural Life, Cobtree Manor Park, Lock Lane, Sandling, Maidstone, Kent ME14 3AU. Telephone: 0622 63936.

Museum of Lincolnshire Life, The Old Barracks, Burton Road, Lincoln LN1 3LY. Telephone: 0522 528448.

Norfolk Rural Life Museum, Beech House, Gressenhall, East Dereham, Norfolk NR20 4DR. Telephone: 0362 860563.

Somerset Rural Life Museum, Abbey Farm, Chilkwell Street, Glastonbury, Somerset BA6 8DB. Telephone: 0458 32903.

Staffordshire County Museum, Shugborough, Stafford ST17 0XB. Telephone: 0889 881388.

Townend, Troutbeck, Windermere, Cumbria LA23 1LB. Telephone: 05394 32628. National Trust.

Welsh Folk Museum, St Fagans, Cardiff, South Glamorgan CF5 6XB. Telephone: 0222 569441.